FOOTPRINTS
OF PAIN AND JOY

Dear Marione — I remember the days of Faith Chapel — I trust God will get you through this grief and I know He will! I know the pain and grief but I also know the comfort God brings.

Hey Billy

HENRY M. PHILLIPS

ISBN 978-1-63814-076-4 (Paperback)
ISBN 978-1-63814-077-1 (Digital)

Covenant Books, Inc.
11661 Hwy 707
Murrells Inlet, SC 29576
www.covenantbooks.com

Introduction

Have you ever been in a situation where you had a friend and when he or she would come by the house to see you, you would try to escape them or avoid them for a number of reasons, of which none made any sense? You did not want them to know you were home. That's what it was like for me when Christ would come to my heart's door, and I would try to find a place to hide or I would avoid Him; I didn't want to answer the door (Rev. 3:20). I felt He would spoil my day with religion or guilt for something I did wrong in my past. Through a series of events and some very rough seas, the day of reconciling came. God made Himself known (it was not the first time). After so many things went wrong, God slowly made Himself known to me, and finally, the load was just too heavy to bear and I fully surrendered to Him. I almost gave up but not until I realized that God meant me no harm, just the opposite; He had my best interests at heart from the very beginning. No matter how I ignored His promptings and his call on my life, He allowed things to happen, and my life, from that moment on, changed...forever! I have never been the same since, and I will never be the same again!

Chapter 1

She Is Dead, Daddy, She Is Dead!

It was early morning and I was driving to work. I had just been assigned a teaching position at Madison County High School as their new JROTC (Junior Reserve Officer Training Course) instructor in Gurley, Alabama. I had to go by Buckhorn High School initially to check in, since my senior JROTC instructor was assigned there, and I needed to check in with him before going to my new assignment. On my arrival to Buckhorn, I received a phone call from my daughter, Sarah, in Washington State, and she said, "Daddy, she is dead. Suzie is dead!"

At the time I was receiving the call, the paramedics were administering a procedure called pericardiocentesis, where they place a needle in her heart to try and remove excess fluid around her heart. To no avail, my little girl was gone! Just weeks earlier, she had given birth to a healthy boy, Maurice. She had placed Maurice on the floor just prior to going into the restroom where she collapsed. I will return to this incident in more detail later but would like to first introduce myself and my family and give some history that leads up to where I am today and hopefully bring some insights into how God brought me through this horrific tragedy.

I was born Henry Monroe Phillips Jr. on January 31, 1945, into a family of eight siblings. My father was paralyzed from his legs down when my grandfather kicked him in his lower back when he was just an infant. I was his namesake, and I really loved my dad very much, especially during the Christmas holidays when he would build a small city in our living room with trains, mountains, and little people skating on a small lake he made out of an old mirror. He was just a genius!

My mother, Margaret, was a victim of infantile paralysis, and in those days, people who were crippled married crippled people—if they got married at all! Crippled people, because that is what they were called, were similar to the untouchables in the Indian culture today. The bottom of the food chain!

Even though my dad and mom have passed many years, I still have a lasting love for them, although my older siblings may have a slightly different view, my parents could do no wrong.

My dad, as much as I loved him, never taught me how to be a man or what a man should be and how we should act in society. There was no teaching on finances, never talked about the birds and the bees, and later in life, as you will read later on, how I wished he had visited those topics with me.

The Bible was rarely, if ever, read in our home as a family, and I cannot remember any of us children reading it on a regular basis. We did, however, attend a little Quaker church just round the corner from my house on occasional Sundays. I remember vividly asking Jesus into my life as a young child around the age of eight or nine, and I do remember attending Vacation Bible School at our elementary school in the summer. My first Bible verse I memorized was Hebrew 4:16, "Let us therefore come boldly to the throne of Grace that we might obtain mercy and find Grace in the time of need." Unfortunately, I did not have a friend who would come alongside me and help me with the newfound faith, and it eventually fell by the wayside. I was extremely shy and pretty much kept to myself most of my young childhood. In spite of my shortcomings, God heard me and I believe now that He had taken personal interest in me. God was not finished with me yet! He still is not as we will find out more…read on!

I was number six in the family pecking order, stuck between two younger sisters and three older brothers and two older sisters! I did not want to hang with sisters for obvious reasons and my older brothers did want little Henry hanging around all the time, so I decided to just be somewhat of a loner!

We lived approximately two miles from Lake Washington, which is a twenty-four-mile lake, and every summer, almost every day, I would hike to that lake and swim all day. I remember my dad teaching me how to swim. Although my dad had legs that never would respond to him, he could outswim fish! I was on the dock and Dad said, "Henry, come here."

I did and he threw me in the lake, I began to paddle like crazy, all the while sinking, and eventually, my dad would reach down and grab me and pull me up for air and then just drop me again! I was not sure that was a form of child abuse, but I did learn to swim!

I would wander through the neighborhood, visiting friends, and one in particular was like a brother to me, Ernie Lewis! After making my neighborhood rounds, I would return home at lunch, eat, and head back out! Sometimes, I would eat at my friend's house because they normally had food, we were poor and we did eat, but nothing like many of my friends ate. Eight kids on welfare and not much food in the house, but we seemed to have made it pretty well. I was in my own little world, and I loved it as long as I was home at a reasonable hour; things were great. I was in my own little world, and I loved it!

I do not remember much of my youth when it comes to my siblings, but I do remember my brother Frank who came home on leave from the Marine Corps and did he look sharp in that uniform and his buddy Ernie too. I thought, *I want to be just like that when I get older.* My sister Norma was distant from me, but she, too, had her boyfriends and eventually married and started having babies. My brother Jim cussed like a sailor but eventually became one of the most impactful men in my life after his conversion to Christianity. When I heard that Jim got saved, I thought this God he came in contact with must be out of His mind! More on Jim later! Bob was distant, too, but he had a friend named Bloss, a Filipino who could cook like no one else, and I fell in love with rice and soy sauce and still love it to this day. Mary was next, and she was kind of a fun-loving person, outgoing, and she ended up marrying a Filipino named

Ernie Silverio, and his brother married my other sister, Shirley. Wow! How crazy. Then the baby, Rose, married and I pretty much kept to myself.

The most significant thing I remember about Shirley and Rose is that they were rascals and would rat on me when I did something I should not have done, for example, in our home you did not just help yourself to food without first checking in with Momma! Well, I was really hungry and decided to snitch a sandwich, so I very meticulously put a peanut butter and jelly sandwich together and carefully placed it in my pocket and began to exit the back door when I heard this familiar voice, "Henry!"

"Yes, Mom."

"Come here."

I stood before my mom, and she asked me what I had in my pocket. I, of course, said nothing, but the bulging pocket spoke for itself, and she asked me to put my hand in my pocket! I very meticulously placed my hand in my pocket; she grabbed my hand and squeezed tightly and then said, "Take your hand out of your pocket."

Without recourse, I did, and you could see the jelly and peanut butter stuck between my fingers; the whipping was worse than the embarrassment of watching my other siblings laughing at me. I learned my lesson, and that was the last time I remember ever taking anything without my mom's permission. I, for some reason, never forgot that incident and have made restitution with my sisters some fifty years later! I love them both now!

I was always in the hospital every summer for some small injury. Rock fights, small cuts, large cuts, I pretty much beat myself up during the summer months. There was a grocery store at the corner of the street north of our home, and I would sneak in and steal candy bars, not knowing that Mr. Panzeka was watching. He never said a word; he just put the price of the item on my mother's bill, and that lasted about a month because when she got her bill and asked Mr. Panzeka about it, yep! You guessed it! I got my backside attended too! It was a nasty habit, but stealing things was something I did a lot when I was younger. I never could afford anything, so I just took things from others. I eventually had that habit broken a few years later!

Chapter 2

School

It was kindergarten and my mom was dropping me off at school, and I remember crying but not too much. I had no idea of what school was all about, and coming from a poor family environment only made matters worse. Personal hygiene was the last thing on my list of fun things to do in life, like shower, brushing my teeth, those kinds of things.

I made it through the first and second and third grades, but fourth grade was a little unusual. As I mentioned earlier, I came from a low-poverty, low-income home, so we did not always have money for clothes or shoes, and my fourth grade teacher would take me up to a restroom and make me wash my feet. All I got out of that was how good a feeling it was to have my feet washed, so I looked forward to it! But I never really developed a personal hygiene regimen! I was not an academic achiever either. I really had problems reading and read on a second-grade level until I was twenty-eight years old. I had no help at home reading; Dad was always gone, and Mom couldn't read much better than I could! My sixth grade was my worst year, but I failed the sixth grade and ended up repeating it and was placed in a special education class. That was the worst experience I ever had, and I promised myself I would never get into another special education class again, and I didn't; however, reading was always a difficult thing for me, and I avoided it like a plague.

Our neighborhood was predominantly White and Oriental when I was five years old; by the time I was ten, it was predominantly

Black. Many of my childhood friends were Black and Asian. I never gave one thought to racial discrimination. One day, I was walking home with some guys from school, and as we were walking, one of them got the bright idea to challenge me to beating up a girl named Bonnie, who was walking home across the street from where we were walking. They said, "We bet you cannot beat up Bonnie."

I said, "Sure I can."

They said, "We dare you."

I said, "Sure, I can beat her up."

We continued walking, and they continued saying, "We double-dog dare you."

Well, those were fighting words for sure. Bonnie was a tomboy, and I thought I would give her the benefit of the doubt and gave her a warning; after all, she is a girl!

"Hey, Bonnie," I yelled, "I am going to beat you up."

She started running, and I started my pursuit, and after two blocks, I still had not caught up with her. She darted down an alley, and I finally caught up with her in front of a bus stop. The bus had just pulled into the stop, and I tackled Bonnie. I was careful not to hurt her because thoughts of my dad ran through my head, and if he knew I was beating up a girl, he would kill me. I turned her over to hit her, and as I drew back, there were repetitious blows to the back my head. I got up, not sure what it was, and to my surprise, there was this sixty-five-year-old woman beating me over the head with an umbrella. I jumped up and took off; I never fought another girl after that! The next day at school, Bonnie had already spread the news of what happened, and for four miserable months, I had taken one tongue-lashing after another from the fellas; it was the most painful time of my life. My ego had been shattered!

I had few friends, but my closest buddy was a guy named Ernie Lewis. I was the guy that adopted his family, even though they may not have adopted me! I was having fun daydreaming in school, and my D and E averages were witness to that fact! As I mentioned earlier, I was a slow learner; my siblings tried helping me, but I just did not have it in me, or if I did, I was not interested in reading or studying. However, the one thing I really enjoyed was playing baseball, usually just hitting rocks with sticks, but I really enjoyed it. Summers were the most fun for the exception of one particular summer at the beach! I was running in the parking lot at Madrona Beach and tripped and slid into a car; in those days, some of the cars had door handles that opened like old refrigerators at one end. I slid and drove my eye into that door handle and spent three weeks in the hospital getting it repaired. The only thing that eased the pain was the moment my sister Mary saw me and she fainted!

I walked everywhere I went; we did not own a car because of my dad and mom's handicap. I walked about 1.5 miles to baseball practice at the Boys' Club. I was the only White kid on the team. I was a very good fielder but a poor hitter, which I attributed to my eye injury. I found out later that if I had considered hitting the ball left-handed, it would have helped a lot, since my dominant eye was my left eye. I tried figuring out just how far I walked as a child—from elementary school to middle school to high school, plus my summer adventures down to Puget Sound—and came up with just over ten thousand miles; this did not include baseball and football practices. I was a patrol boy in elementary school, helping other kids cross busy streets. I had just come in from my afternoon duties when a teacher said the principal wanted to see me and that it was important. I went to the office, and he sat me down and told me that my dad had passed away that morning. I ran all the way home, weeping as I ran but not really understanding why. My mom suggested that I not attend the funeral because she felt it was just too much for me, but I really did not understand what was happening. He would be really missed at Christmastime when he would construct the miniature towns and railroads, but I seemed to allow that tragedy to pass without too much harm. I loved my dad and would miss him but realized that life goes on and you just cannot bring those you love back.

Middle School

I walked to middle school, Washington Junior High, every day, rain or shine, hot or cold, approximately 1.8 miles from my home. My dad played a really good trumpet and, at one time, tried out for the Benny Goodman band, but because he was crippled, he did not make it! I thought I would try the trombone, and for three years, I enjoyed my time in band. My parents never attended any of my base-ball games or other school activities, except my mom did come to one band performance and to my Eagle Scout presentation. I never felt bad about that; actually, I understood their physical handicap, and I never took it personally.

Middle school was really a bad experience for me because of a kid named Tommy Morris, a heavyset Black kid who constantly harassed me, calling me "rich boy" when in reality I rarely had any money on me at all. I was always broke, but the harassment came almost every day, and I spent most of my days escaping and evading Tommy. I was bullied and never was one to want to fight anyone. There was one highlighted experience I will never forget. One day at lunch, I was sitting next to a girl named Brodianne, a tomboy, and she was tough, but we got along just fine. Across from Brodianne, Tommy sat down, and when Brodianne turned away, temporarily distracted by a friend, Tommy put some mashed potatoes in her purse. She reached across the table and hit Tommy so hard you could see the excess weight on him just wobble. I thought, *I am going to marry that girl.* We became even closer friends. Middle school was over, and high school was just around the corner.

High School

There was one very special art teacher, Mrs. Olsen, who loved the Phillips family. I remember doing a piece of art for an art show, and another teacher purchased it for $15, and I thought I was rich. Art was my favorite subject not because of the money I won but because of a wonderful, caring teacher who saw in Henry something he did not see in himself. I was in high school marching band for two years and decided I wanted to do sports. I ran cross-country, did pole vaulting, and tried out for the football team. I began to buff up some, and by the time I was a junior in high school, I was six feet and three inches tall and weighed 185 pounds. I was fast and had made the varsity football team. My friend Mike Palmer was also a trombone player—better than I was—and a really good football player as well, and he kept harassing me about playing football. He would ask me when I was going to get out of that monkey suit and put on a real uniform. I regret putting up the trombone even to this day, but when your ego calls, normally you answer, and I did! My football coach, John Botano, was tough but fair, and I liked him a lot; he told me, along with the other players, that we all had three options:

1. You can drink if you like.
2. You can chase the girls if you like.
3. You can play football for me, but options 1 and 2 are off the table.

In spring practice my senior year, I caught my first and only touchdown; later that spring, another family tragedy happened. I was at home and I heard my mother groaning. I went down to see what the matter was, and she said she needed some water. I immediately went to the kitchen and got her a glass of water. Things did not improve, so one of my older siblings called for an ambulance. On the way to the hospital, my mom passed away, and I did not attend her funeral either. Our family was dispersed among my older sisters, and the youngest, Rose, went to stay with Mary, along with Shirley. Mary had been married and was living in California; her husband was in the Navy. I had an aunt and uncle living in Tacoma, Washington, whom I visited with in the summer months on occasion. They wanted me to come and live with them and attend school. My uncle Bud was a retired army sergeant, a World War II veteran. He had been shot in the mouth, and the round came out the back of his neck, but he survived. My football career was put on hold until I attended a new high school, Lincoln High School, in Tacoma, Washington. A new high school, new faces, new friends—it was scary initially.

Lincoln was a predominantly White school; all the Black students would meet in one area, and I would usually meet with them. I started to study and actually began to enjoy it. It was my senior year. One of the things I enjoyed doing was dancing, and I was very good at it, but the White guys didn't like me dancing with the Black girls. The Black didn't like me dancing with them either because on the dance floor, they would flock around me, waiting to get the next dance. Lincoln High School was number 3 in the nation in football, so the competition was exceptionally good. My competition was a guy named Dave Williams, and he ended up playing with the Cardinals! My aunt and uncle did not want me playing football because they thought I would get hurt. I insisted and went out for the team, but the only helmet that was left was one without any padding in it, but I wore it, anyway. It was not long after practice the first day that I had cut my head on a piece of plastic in the helmet. My aunt said, "That's it, no more football."

I started dating out of my race, and my aunt was mortified! My uncle would take me out to Fort Lewis, Washington, and just show me around, probably hoping that I would opt out of school and join the army. My aunt and uncle sat me down and suggested I get a job, and they told me of a possible job opening in downtown Tacoma. They told me how they pay good, that they make you wear store uniforms, and that there are real good opportunities for advancement in the company. I was getting excited until I went to this place of business on 100 Broadway Street and saw above the door to this business was a huge sign that read "United States Army Recruiter." I got the message and went in to apply. I could only read on a second-grade level and had to retake the test twice before finally passing it on a third effort! I figured the army recruiters got together after the second test and decided that the Vietnam War was getting started and that the army could use a few good bullet stoppers; they helped me get the third test passed, and off I went to Fort Ord, California. Before I entered into the military career, let me go back to the most crucial time in my childhood and the most productive.

Chapter 3

Boys Scouts

In 1962, I was awarded the Eagle Scout Award in Troop 209, Seattle, Washington. My brother Jim had somehow come in contact with scouting and encouraged me to join. I did not have the money to pay for uniforms, but someone did, and it was a great investment for them and for me. If you remember me telling you I had this habit of stealing things when I was younger, and I did not think taking my scoutmaster's car for a spin would come under the heading of stealing even though I did not have his permission. I had walked down to Madrona Beach and saw a bike in the lake. I got in and pulled the bike out and cleaned it off and rode it home. As I was riding around the block, in front of Ernie's home, his mom, Ruby, a precious and wonderful lady, said to me, "Henry, where did you steal that bike?"

Humiliated and with the thought that I was recognized as a thief, I decided to return the bike to the lake and throw it back in. I never did steal again…well!

I was doing some work at my scoutmaster's home, and he was at work. He had an old Buick sitting out in front of his house, and I figured he wouldn't mind if I took it for a ride, so I got in; the keys were in it, so I decided to take it for a ride. I had no idea what I was doing! I knew my numbers and letters and put the gear shift into D for drive, I knew that much, but what I did not know was that the emergency brake was a floor brake and that if I pressed it in, it would release the brake. I started moving forward but a little slower than normal and drove it about three miles near my girlfriend's house. I stopped on the wrong side of the street to get some water to put in the radiator because there was so much smoke. I got out of the car and went across the street to the gas station, while my girlfriend and sister stayed by the car. A police officer drove up and asked who the car belonged to, and they said one of those men across the street at the gas station; there were five or six men there besides me. The cop told my sister to make sure the man gets the car moved, and he drove off! I got back into the car and started back home—oh, by the way, the emergency brake was still on! Duh! As I was driving back, I looked out the back window and saw there was smoke everywhere. I looked like a hydroplane on Lake Washington during Seafair with this huge rooster tail behind me. I finally got back to the corner of the scoutmaster's home, and I heard this huge pop, and the back of the car dropped. How was I going to move this car to the front of the scoutmaster's home? I went home and found a neighbor who could help me push the car in front of the house and then headed home and waited for the fireworks to begin…and they did! The scoutmaster, obviously upset, was ready to call the cops and send me to the detention center, or D-home as they called it! My stepdad would have put me in the D-home for sure, but the scoutmaster had a different idea. Thanks to my older brother Jim, I would work off the $600 for repairs on the car. I mowed his yard all summer, painted his house inside and out, and never stole another thing in my life. I was sure glad to hear that the Boy Scouts did not give out merit badges for car theft!

Scouting saved my life in the long run. I learned so much from that organization that I attribute much of my success in the military to scouting. I will always be eternally grateful to the Scouts!

Scouting took me into the mountains, taught me leadership skills, map reading, and navigation, and I was a happy kid as a result of becoming an Eagle Scout and of all the activities that my mom came to as a child and I could count them on three fingers, coming to my awards ceremony for Eagle Scout had to be one the happiest moments for her and for me before her passing.

Chapter 4

You're in the Army Now!

Prior to joining the army, I met a beautiful Japanese-African-American girl named Keiko and fell in love, whatever that is! I had no idea what love and marriage were about! I did not write her because I was off to basic, and all the rumors about having no time to write made me concentrate more on becoming a soldier. I joined the army on September 23, 1963, and I was so naïve and innocent and never thought about being a godly man, had no idea what that was; there were plenty of good men but not many godly men.

Leaving Seattle-Tacoma Airport, we flew south to California and Fort Ord. After my flight, which I thought was really cool, I boarded a bus with several other guys, and we drove to the fort. We took our physicals and I passed with flying colors. I did well with all the physical stuff; that was easy. What was not easy was the reading requirements along the way. During the seventh week of basic training, I was on KP (Kitchen Patrol); you know pots and pans, grease pit, dishes, etc. I scored highest in administrative skills (would you believe that); at the end of basic, I headed to AIT (Advanced Individual Training) and spent eight to twelve hours a day, typing every day for eight weeks. At the end of the eight weeks, I could type thirty-five words a minute and was worth my weight in gold to some first sergeant who needed a good company clerk. Besides the school training, there were still the additional duties of kitchen patrol and guard duty. I completed my advanced individual training, and now I would receive my first full-time duty assignment at Fort Knox, Kentucky. I was put to work in a reception station; that's a place where new troops would come in from all over the country for basic training in armor; that's tanks. I would type up their ID cards and other appropriate paperwork needed for processing the new troops into basic tank training. I had played sports in high school and I enjoyed being active, and typing up ID cards was not something I thought I would like to do the rest of my life, so I decided to go to jump school or airborne training! Sometimes, your ego gets the best of you, and I always wanted to please others and was willing to do almost anything to satisfy my ego! I submitted my paperwork for jump school, and approximately one month later, I was on a bus to the United States Army Airborne School!

As I neared Fort Benning, Georgia, I could see these huge towers, 250-foot towers, and wondered just what did I get myself into? Before training began, I spent the first week on kitchen patrol in the Officer's Candidate School. After that first exciting week, the training began! Wow! Who is this guy in my face telling me to drop (the term used for getting down and doing ten pushups)! I must have done five thousand pushups during that first week alone. Everywhere you went you had to run; if you went to the Post Exchange, you would have to run, buy what you needed, and run back to the barracks. We began by running five miles every morning, down around the airfield and back to the company area.

The first week of training, they put you in these harnesses and pushed you off an elevated platform and then dropped you, and you had to land on your feet, thighs, roll on your shoulders; they called it a PLF (Parachute Landing Fall). Then came the fifty-foot towers; they attached a harness to you, stood you in front of the simulated aircraft door, and pushed you out. Here you learned the right technique to exit an aircraft, the proper position to prepare for your chute to deploy, and you would have to count to four and then look up and check your risers to make sure your chute would fully deploy, but you were actually attached to a cable where you would bounce about one hundred yards and the drill sergeants would make you get out of the harness and run back to the tower.

Week two of airborne training consisted of your normal five-mile run in the morning along with what was referred to as the daily dozen which consisted of twelve exercises that you would have to complete first before the run! After PT (physical training), we were headed for the 250-foot towers; that's a long way up, but it looks a lot higher from the top than it does from the bottom. They put you in a harness and raised you up 250 feet, then they would pop a lever, and you would be on your own, floating down to earth, and you would have to maneuver the parachute and land safely on the ground using your instructions for a good parachute landing fall! It made no difference what rank you were, from general to private, you dropped when the drill sergeants told you to! The second week ended, and our final week was jump week; this is when we actually jumped out of an airplane! We were required to make five jumps: four regular jumps and one equipment jump. We gathered at the airfield and loaded the aircraft, a lot of excitement during this time, and I remember so vividly the man who was jumping behind me was a US Army chaplain. I had no idea what a chaplain was, but I found out he was like a preacher in civilian life, Chaplain Smith, a Southern Baptist chaplain, so I took the liberty to ask him to pray for me and he said, "Sure, glad to!"

That was my first encounter with a chaplain! I did not know a lot about God nor was I necessarily interested in Him, but whatever that chaplain prayed, it probably was more than just keep the young soldier safe in this jump. Later in my military career, to my amazement, the chaplains played a major role in my life!

There was one young soldier who got his ripcord tangled around his neck and jumped out of the plane before he could untangle it, and it burned a nasty mark on his neck! Those who made mistakes were sent to the "chicken farm"; it was a two-story barracks building, and they were labeled legs! The best part of a chicken is the leg! So all those who do not have jump wings in the military are referred to as legs! On graduation day after our last jump, we all got into a company formation and our wings were pinned on by our company commander and we were now airborne soldiers! Hooah!

During jump school, I noticed these soldiers with funny little hats they called berets! They looked sharp, and I inquired how you get those hats, and they said to sign up for a unit called Special Forces, hmmm! Sounded good to me, so I put in my paperwork while in jump school and my next assignment would be in Headquarters Company, 5th Special Forces Group (Airborne), 1st Special Forces, Fort Bragg, North Carolina!

These airborne units prided themselves on looking sharp, clean uniforms, badges on uniforms neat and clean, boots polished really nice, and I took a personal pride in knowing that my uniform was always immaculate. I would now have to make mandatory parachute jumps every three months to retain my airborne status, and I enjoyed it immensely! I want to make sure that you understand that I was not a school-trained Special Forces soldier. I served in an administrative role, supporting Special Forces. Although not school trained, I did have a lot of respect for those who were SF qualified.

I was a very shy person, kept to myself, stayed out of trouble; after all, I was only eighteen years old! A lot of soldiers in the administrative field had some level of college, and I was a high-school dropout! I had no ambition to go to school, and it was pretty intimidating to keep asking others how to spell words or correct notes I was typing for someone. Speaking of being naïve, I was on the top floor of a double-decker barracks and was a good athlete; most good athletes were assigned to headquarters company because they could play sports as well as work, and some units would recruit athletes when they came through the in-processing procedures because almost all of the recruits would come through headquarters! They wanted to stack the deck in hopes to win unit sports awards. I was coming back to the barracks after work one day, and the sergeant said to me, "Phillips, come here!"

He asked me if I would be interested in playing softball, and I said sure! He told me they were having a game at seven o'clock that evening and to be at the park at 6:00 p.m. I showed up ready to play, and one of the guys on our team was acting really sporadic, almost as if he were short a few marbles, if you know what I mean! He would jump on the backstop and climb up like a chimp at a zoo, then he would get a bat and start hitting the dugout, like this boy needs some serious medical help. After the game, I returned to the barracks, and this guy slept right across from me on the upper floor. The sergeant asked if he could see me for a moment, so I went to see what he wanted, and he told me that this guy was once assigned to Charlie Company and had been in an underwater accident. He had set some explosives, and they went off prematurely as he was swimming away from the site.

There had been a couple of murders in Bravo and Charlie Companies, but they could never find the culprit. He told me that those who were murdered were severely beaten by an entrenching tool: that's a small shovel used by troops to dig holes on field exercises. He further suggested that if he should get up early in the morning and start searching for his entrenching tool that would be in his foot-locker, that I should get up out of bed and head for the shower, jump in, and turn the water on because he had such a fear of water due to his experience with planting those explosives underwater. At 3:00 a.m., I heard this rumbling across from my bunk, and sure enough, this guy was up looking for his entrenching tool, and I headed for the showers, jumped in, turned the water on, and he followed me into the shower but would not get in while the water was running. I was close to terrified by now.

Two sergeants show up and calm him down and then tell me he is going to be okay and for me to go back to bed! Sure I will. I got no sleep that night, and the next morning while I was at work, we all worked in the same area, one desk behind the other with the NCOIC (noncommissioned officer in charge) at the head of the room. I went up to him and asked him if he would allow me to see the company commander because I felt this guy needed medical treatment, and as I turned around, everyone in the office just burst out with laughter. I had been taken hook, line, and sinker! When other non-commissioned officers got the drift that I was so naïve, they decided to play with me even more, so one day, one of the NCOs told me to go to other companies to find some pink carbon paper; in those days, there was only black carbon paper, but I knew this!

I started out my search and decided to go the command sergeant major's office and ask for some pink carbon paper that Sergeant Billingsley sent me to find. I entered his office and his secretary met me and asked me what I wanted, and when I told her what I was there for, she seemed really puzzled and yet chuckled some. She called the sergeant major on the intercom and she told him what I was there for! He asked me to come into his office, and so I entered, and he asked me what I wanted, then asked to repeat it again. I did! He said, "Who sent you up here?"

I gave him the sergeant's name, and he told me to take a seat, and we waited as he called down to my office and asked for Sergeant Billingsley. It was not long before Sergeant Billingsley showed up and the sergeant major asked him what he had asked me to get; when he told the sergeant major, the sergeant major tore into him so bad, I even started to cry! He told Sergeant Billingsley to forget his plans for the weekend, that he would be picking up pinecones on post all weekend long! Amazing, from that moment on, no other sergeants bothered me to do little errands for them any longer. You just do not mess with the sergeant major.

Chapter 5

Vietnam, Tour One

In November 1964, the group commander called the unit to the theater and informed us that our unit was going to Vietnam, and a few weeks later, we were packed and ready to go. There was this soldier in one of the line companies by the name of Barry Sadler who wrote this song called the "Green Berets," which became very popular, and many young men joined the unit as a result of that song. John Wayne's movie *The Green Berets* was also incentive for many young men to sign up! Real Green Beret soldiers were nothing like the movies portray them; these men are intelligent, bust their bottoms, know what they are doing, are dedicated, and in the truest sense of the word, professionals! I remember arriving at Tan Son Nhut Air Base in Saigon and really not aware of what was in my future! I was assigned to 5th Group Headquarters TOC (Tactical Operations Center) as intelligence clerk, typing up situation reports from the field. I am still reading on a second grade level, and it was extremely difficult for me to comprehend the military language or jargon, so I decided to run and requested an MOS (Military Occupational Specialty) change (MOS is just a military term for a job specification). I thought I could do better in supply and logistics: I could count well, I knew the different sizes of clothing and foot gear, I could load supplies on trucks and airplanes, and so I switched. I still had to type things for the supply sergeant, but it beat typing situation reports.

Remember, I am only eighteen years old, still very damp behind the ears, and the supply sergeant asked me to drive an 18-wheeler from the docks on the Saigon River to the airfield. I said, "Sure."

I just received my driver's license and was not totally aware of road signs, not international roads signs anyway. I reported to the dock, got into the truck, which was automatic, thank God, and began driving toward the airport. As I left the dock, I noticed this red circular sign with a white line through it and thought maybe I will go up that street, and as I turned my truck up that street, everyone was coming in my direction and shaking their fists and probably cussing me out in Vietnamese. Finally, after a few blocks, the "white mice," as we called the police, pulled me over and told me that I was traveling on a one-way street, the wrong way! I immediately took the next right and then got back on track and made it safely to the airport.

Our quarters in Saigon were in a hotel, and it was really nice living quarters. We had a small zoo out back with two rock pythons, one eight feet and the other five feet long. Four small monkeys, a lizard that was about four feet long, and a small deer! In our spare time, we could go into the city, and my peers introduced me to alcohol and women. I was never much of a drinker or womanizer, but sometimes, the influence of others makes you try things you wish you never had; it is called peer pressure and it's real!

Sergeant Billingsley invited me to town for an introduction to Vietnamese culture that really turned out to be just a time of drinking and carousing. Later that evening, on our way home, we were going to take what we called a cyclo (pronounced *sick-low*) home; it was a three-wheeled, foot-pedaled tricycle with a seat up front for at least two guys and pedaled by a little Vietnamese guy. We decided to take two cyclos. Sergeant Billingsley would ride one and I would ride the other. I had not been in country for three days. I could pedal a bike but had no idea how to operate the cyclo, so guided by my ego, we started pedaling home or back to the hotel. As we picked up speed, we had no idea how to stop the cyclo! Sergeant Billingsley found a small lever under his seat and thought, *I will just pull this up and see what happens.* He did and the cyclo stopped almost immediately, and the little cyclo driver flew out the front end and I was quite sure he was upset, and although I did not know the language, I am sure I got my first grammar lesson on Vietnamese profanity! I did not actually see how Sergeant Billingsley tried to stop his cyclo, so I decided to do things a little different. I would, in my bright mind, pull the cyclo over to the curve and stop by friction! When I did, the cyclo jack-knifed, and the little driver flew out the front of the cyclo and I went over the top! I got my second grammar lesson on Vietnamese profanity, I'm sure! We decided to pay the little Vietnamese drivers a little extra for their trouble and damages; they were satisfied, and we went on our way.

On the way into the compound where we were housed, Sergeant Billingsley thought it was a great idea to play with the animals, but I had had enough excitement for one evening. I headed to bed. Shortly after I got in bed, I could hear Sergeant Billingsley out in the hallway; it sounded as if he were choking! I got up but so did the sergeant major, and we found Sergeant Billingsley out in the hallway with the eight-foot python around his neck, and so we got the snake off him and the sergeant major said a few words to Sergeant Billingsley that I am not at liberty to say here and told Sergeant Billingsley to put the snake back in its cage. Sergeant Billingsley left with the snake, and the SGM returned to his room and me to mine. I had been in bed maybe fifteen minutes when I felt something very weird on my legs as if something were crawling in my bed. I immediately jumped up, turned the sheets over, and there was Sergeant Billingsley pushing that snake up under my sheets. I told him he had better put the snake back. Sometimes when you are too inebriated to think straight, you end up doing really stupid things, but the night was far from over. Sergeant Billingsley returned the snake to its cage, but after he put the snake down for the night, he noticed the monkey cage and thought it would be a nice idea to let them out! He did, and the colonel's office was just feet away from the monkey cage and the window to his office was slightly opened. Sergeant Billingsley left the monkey alone and returned to his room for the night! About four o'clock in the morning, you could hear the colonel yelling in the court yard, "Sergeant Billingsley!"

It took the SGM to get Sergeant Billingsley out of bed and presentable for the colonel. The colonel asked Sergeant Billingsley if he had let the monkeys out of their cage; he said, "Yes, sir!"

He continued to blast Sergeant Billingsley because the monkeys not only got out but lifted the windows to the colonel's office and literally destroyed everything. The colonel suggested that Sergeant Billingsley get the monkeys back into their cages. The monkeys were fed well, so they won't go far. Sergeant Billingsley went to his room and got his rifle and took two shots at the monkeys that were in the trees, hoping to scare them back into their cage. Duh? The SGM heard the rounds and got Sergeant Billingsley in the courtyard and, again, chewed his first layer of flesh off and then told him to pack his bags; he was on his way to the jungle! The SGM said, "If you want to shoot, we will let you shoot, pack your bags, and pick up your orders," and he was sent out into the field to finish his tour.

I never heard from Sergeant Billingsley again! I know this sounds a little far-fetched, but I am eyewitness to this type of stupidity that started the night before with a drunken stupor. I learned more about drinking and was a much more conservative drinker from then on. There were some guys from a Christian mission who came to visit me just after I left for town with Sergeant Billingsley, and I have always wondered how things would have gone if those men would have caught me before I went to town.

I requested to leave Saigon and go to 5th Special Forces Group in Nha Trang as a supply and logistics specialist. I would handle all sorts of supplies. I would fly on resupply missions to A, B, and C detachments, dropping supplies from the back of aircraft. It was a lot more fun than the hotel accommodations in Saigon; besides, I was outside more and moved around a lot! During my last few months of my first tour in Vietnam, we were on a resupply mission, and we had stored all the supplies on the aircraft. We had a pig that was put into a bamboo container, and you twisted the opened end of the container to secure the pig. We were coming in for the drop, the tail gate of the aircraft was dropped, and somehow, the pig got out and we chased that pig all through the aircraft, but to no avail; the little critter ran right out of the back of the airplane, and we could see it drop from 250 feet. One thing I can attest to is that without a doubt, pigs do not fly!

I enjoyed the last half of my first tour in Vietnam. I returned home and was stationed at Fort Bragg, North Carolina, again. The year was 1965, and I had decided to go into a nearby town, Fayetteville, North Carolina, and party. I did not feel uncomfortable going to a bar that was predominately black because of my childhood neighborhood, but I found out that all black people are not alike, just like all white people are not alike! I began to drink some, and there was this woman who wanted to keep dancing with me and so I did, but something just did not feel right. I decided to go back to the barracks. The following day, Sunday, I decided to go to chapel or church in civilian language. I never had been to chapel except one time in basic when all the troops were required at least once to attend chapel. The sermon was okay, but I really did not understand much of what was said, so I returned to my barracks and I first entered the orderly room; in the military, there is a small building at the head of each of the barracks where a charge of quarters (CQ) was on duty twenty-four hours. He said to me, "Phillips, come here!"

I came to him, and he said, "There were three men and a woman who came by to see you and wanted to know if you were here, and I told them you had gone to chapel."

He said the guys looked pretty rough and they asked some personal questions I could not answer. I had no idea what a shotgun wedding was, but after talking with the CQ, I got the impression from his description that these people who came to visit had other plans. I got spooked, and since my reenlistment was coming soon and I went to the recruiter and asked for an assignment to Alaska, I figured I would be safe there! It was just a few weeks and my orders came down. I had thirty days of leave and was eager to go.

Chapter 6

My First Marriage

I was an extremely naïve young man, and when I arrived home, I decided to look up this gal I knew in high school. She was really pretty, and I met her at school one day and decided to ask her out; to my surprise, she said yes! She was Japanese and African-American. We started seeing each other, I met her parents, and one thing led to another, and the next thing I knew, I was engaged to be married. I would soon be going to Alaska for my next assignment and so we began to plan the wedding. I would go to Alaska first and then return later; we would marry and return to Fort Greely, Alaska, together. I had played baseball as a kid and got the privilege to play for the Fort Greely Bears; it was like playing on a semi-pro team. We played in Fairbanks one season against the Fairbank wolves and beat them 7–2; it was the highlight of my baseball career. I also enjoyed drill team and color guard, and one time after we performed for a ceremony, my wife at that time asked me what it was I was doing, and I told her I was in the Color Guard, and her response was, "You're not colored!" I explained to her later that day. Colors are flags, not a race!

I was on the run again; we were happy for a while. I attended the NCO Academy at Fort Wainwright, Alaska. I worked in a nuclear power plant and a gym and then I decided to go back to Vietnam, not knowing that my wife was pregnant with our first child. I had no idea how to manage money, and it would plague me for nearly all of my life. I was in debt, and the extra $55 for jump pay and combat pay seemed to be a way for me to get ahead of my debt. I headed for Vietnam, and my wife went back to her parents' home in Tacoma, Washington. We kept in touch, we wrote a lot, and we met in Hawaii for leave and enjoyed that time together.

My Second Tour in Vietnam

When I arrived in Vietnam, I was asked if I would like to be on the cadre of the MACV (Military Assistance Command Vietnam). Recondo School! And my ego jumped at it; as I interviewed with the sergeant major, he told me I would first have to go through the training even though I was just their supply sergeant, it was mandatory to do the training in order to be cadre at the school. Three weeks of tough training. I was driving my jeep in the city of Nha Trang and noticed the Christian Servicemen's Center; the word *Christian* stuck out, and I thought I would investigate. I stopped in for a moment and visited with a man named Lem Morgan and his wife Marge; they were missionaries. After talking with them, I returned to my barracks at the Recondo School, and later, the next week, I started my three-week training:

Week 1: Up in the morning for PT, then a thirty-pound bag of sand was put in my back pack: all of my LBE (load-bearing equipment), which included two canteens of water, two ammunition pouches with five magazines total, twenty rounds in each pouch, a bayonet, compass, and blood plasma. Day 1, we would walk at the fastest speed we could for one week; we would eventually, at the end of the week, have to speed walk for seven miles and make it in one hour and fifteen minutes in order to qualify. If you could not make it, you could not continue in the program and some were sent back to their units. During the first week, we also had to learn how to operate a field radio, learn how to read a map, and use it in the field. We also had to give ourselves a shot in the arm just in case we were injured in the field; we had to be able to administer the blood plasma. We also had to give another soldier a shot in the arm, and during the class, all the US troops had been paired up and the only guy left for me was a Korean soldier. He could not speak English and I could not speak

Korean, and when it came my turn to stick him in the arm with the needle, it went really smooth, but when it became his turn, he kept trying to put the needle in and it wasn't going well, so I called the Korean liaison officer over and told him to tell the soldier to put the needle in my arm; he did and I could have sworn that needle went all the way through my body and out my other arm. One thing about the Koreans that you have to appreciate is their attention to orders, and when that Korean officer spoke to that private, he did exactly as he was told, unfortunately to my expense!

Week 2: We continue wearing our load-bearing equipment and continued our physical training. We started on the fifty-five foot towers and we climbed up a rope ladder on one side of the tower and rappelled down the other side of the tower. It took a few days to get everyone through this, but we also learned about different weapons and how to fire them. On the fourth day, we went out in the field, and we climbed a rope ladder up thirty feet into a helicopter and then back down; after that we got into the helicopter and ascended 120 feet and rappelled down to the ground. Some soldiers just didn't pay attention, and as they exited the chopper, they put pressure on the guide hand and fell forward, hitting their heads on the struts of the chopper; some knocked themselves out, others just got a bad headache, I survived! The last big event of the day was to get into what was called a McQuire rig; it was a hundred feet of three-fourths-inch nylon rope dangling from a chopper; there were three eye loops at the bottom. I was in the middle and two other soldiers were to my left and right. The chopper began moving around the valley, and we were just dangling from the chopper. These techniques of rope ladders and McQuire rigs were used in the field if troops needed to be evacuated from the jungle. That was the last time that type of evacuation technique was used, and I was fortunate enough to be one of the last guys to use it.

Week 3, Field Exercise: We got up early, it was a Thursday, and we headed out toward the training site that had been used for a whole year, but this time, they decided to switch the sites. We landed the choppers and the troops unloaded and headed for cover. It was getting dark and the radio man laid his rain poncho down just above and to the left of mine. I laid mine down and began to fall asleep when I heard this small voice in my head telling me to turn over, and at first, I just ignored it, but when I heard it a second time, I thought maybe I should follow through, and as I turned over, a bright yellow snake, a bamboo viper, was just a few inches away from me, and one of the other sergeants stepped on it and killed it and informed me that this particular snake, had it bitten me, could have killed me within minutes. I immediately began to think of the Christian Servicemen's Center and what Lem Morgan had shared with me about Jesus. Moments later, we receive machine-gun fire and the radioman calls in for artillery support, "Cowboy 1-8, fire mission over."

The artillery unit has already put our position on their guns, and they began to fire almost spontaneously. The sound of a 105mm Howitzer is pretty deafening; besides, this is my first time being faced with an actual enemy that I could not see. After the Howitzers fired, we just waited for morning to arrive. I could see some shadows moving but did not fire because I was not sure they were friendly or not. I did not want the thought of killing our own soldiers on my conscience. When morning finally came, we saw two or three Vietcong, and a squad of men began to chase them; they followed them into the old Mission Support Site. They changed this site for the first time in a year! Near the area where we normally landed the troops was a 250 pound that had been booby-trapped, and if we had landed there, it would have been fatal for many of us! The squad continued chasing the two VC and returned, and as all of this was taking place, a small aircraft we called FAC (Forward Air Control) was flying above us, and as he spotted the two VC, he called in the F105 and F4 Phantom Jets that were hovering at seven to ten thousand feet and told them to "hit my smoke."

The small FAC would fire a smoke rocket and then, out of the blue, literally, came these beautiful aircraft, and they dropped 2,500-pound bombs on their target and hit an anti-aircraft gun site. All the students were sitting on the ground in an open field watching the fireworks; it was awesome, I must admit! The thing that bothered me more than anything else was the thoughts of going to hell if I died. I knew I would end up in hell, and when I had the opportunity, I returned to the Christian Servicemen's Center and gave my life to Christ. The one thing I wish I would have done was to search out other godly men to help me grow. I just assumed that I was safe and could continue living like I was, but that a simple confession of my faith would keep me out of hell's fire! Was I wrong!

There were a couple of incidents that were more humorous than serious and one took place at the Recondo School; it was in the middle of my tour, and I was in the supply room when I heard this huge explosion and I thought for sure that we were getting overrun, so I got my gear and headed for my post on the perimeter! I exited the front door and another explosion went off, and I hit the ground, looking in every direction to see what was going on! One of the sergeants thought it might be a good idea to put up a 106 recoilless rifle on the perimeter of the compound. Well, he set it up right behind the dining facility which was a brand-new facility. The back blast of a 106 recoilless rifle is approximately 70 meters. He set it up about twenty-five feet, and when the first round went off, it blew the sand bags and corrugated steel down, blew the back door off the new dining facility, and the second round blew the back door off and all the florescent light bulbs fell out of their sockets and the sergeant major was extremely upset, and I am not at liberty to repeat what he said in this book!

Sometimes, men would drink and do some pretty stupid things, and one evening, there was a scuffle and one of the guys broke his leg and the other two were somewhat inebriated, to say the least! They decided to put the injured sergeant in a jeep and take him across the airfield to the hospital. All three of them were snockered! When they arrived, the two friends got the injured man out of the jeep and put him on a gurney and had his feet hanging over the bottom of the gurney, so when they hit the door to enter the hospital, the poor guy's feet hit first and then the yelling began, the cursing began, and the doctor showed up. The doctor wore glasses and the drunken soldier said, "What ——— do you think you are going to do?"

The doctor gently grabbed him by the leg and squeezed, the soldier cried out, and the doctor just said, "Let me know when it hurts!"

The moral of this story is simply do what the doctor tells you to and keep your comments to yourself!

Big Boat, Little Boat!

The commandant at the school was a short guy but big in stature, if you know what I mean! This assignment was a big one because it was the first time we were going to make a water infiltration on an island off the coast of Nha Trang. We boarded a PT boat with two 750-horsepower engines; there were nine of us on the team. We parked the PT boat about 1,500 yards off the coast of the island. Then we boarded, a rubber raft, and myself and one other instructor plus some team members began rowing to shore. We got about 100 yards off shore, and the team leader thought that we were compromised; there were some small boats in the area, and he thought they might be VC, so he calls back to, let's just call it Big Boat and refer to the rubber raft as Little Boat! Team leader gets on the radio and says, "Big Boat, this is Little Boat, over!"

"Go ahead, Little Boat."

"We have been compromised. We are returning to your location."

"Little Boat, this is Big Boat, continue the mission!"

We make a couple of spins in the water, and the team leader calls back again; he called the third time, telling Big Boat that we have been compromised and we are coming back!

Big Boat sends the final message, "I have four 50-caliber guns on this boat, and if you come back, I will blow your —— out of the water!"

We rowed ashore and dropped off the team and myself and one other instructor rowed that rubber raft 1,200 yards back to the boat, and our arms were like spaghetti! We went back a few days later to retrieve the team. It was close to the end of my second tour in Vietnam, and I was ready to get home and see my little daughter, Lisa. But I wanted to go on one more mission and went to see the SGM about going. He told me no, not just no but —— no (expletive is mine). He said, "Did you not just have a baby?" and I said yes.

"Well, you are going home to her."

And I was mad, but he was the sergeant major and you don't argue with the sergeant major unless you have an empty skull! I later found out that this sergeant major had just lost a son in the 101st Airborne Division a few months earlier. I began to think of how selfish I was and started my processing to come home.

Chapter 7

Military, Marriage, and Family

I would like to remind you that when I was younger, I had no male input except some friends who knew nothing about relationships. I could hardly wait to see Lisa; my heart jumped every time I thought of her! Even though I was a Christian by word only, I had not been reading my Bible or anything else, no church, no fellowship, and so this ship soon was drifting at sea! The first thing I did was grab that little girl and, for the next few days, just hugged her! My orders were sending me to Fort Devens, Massachusetts, to the 10th Special Forces Group. I was a supply sergeant in C Company. Just before leaving Tacoma for Massachusetts, I purchased a 1967 Chevy Camaro, and off we went. I was already in debt some and began to get even more in debt and decided to get extra work so I bussed tables for a little while to get extra cash. I was a bouncer at a nightclub outside the post, and I figured I loved her and she loved me, but I had no idea what that kind of love was; it was purely a mixture of covetousness and materialism. She had plans I was unaware of, and I just was very jealous of her—not a good combination.

Now our son, Rick, arrives and I am even more excited, but somehow things just did not seem to get better and I did not know how to fix the leak in the boat. We eventually parted ways, and I got the children in my custody. Having the children in my care was crucial to me even when I had no idea what being a father was! There was some domestic violence, none of which was her fault, and I got my first Article 15 and was busted from the rank of staff sergeant to buck sergeant and was lucky they did not kick me out of the army. I had no education, no idea what I would do, but I needed to take care of the children. I put in for a reassignment to Fort Riley, Kansas, but was there for only a few months before deciding to go back to Vietnam, the third time; what about the kids? I had an older sister in Clay Center, Nebraska, and she was willing to take the kids until I returned. I got the kids packed and settled at my sister's home and headed for Vietnam.

I would go to Seattle first and party and then leave. I felt as if I had failed as father and husband and didn't care if I returned from Vietnam or not! I went to my brother's home first and then rented a car and took off for Seattle and picked up a friend, and we went out, chased the girls, drank, and that was it. I returned to my brother's house, who by the way, was a wonderful Christian man and his wife was just awesome, and I often wondered why my marriage could not have turned out that way! As I entered Jim's house, I was in a really bad mood, no women, just drunk, and he said to me after I shared my disappointing evening with him, "Praise the Lord!"

I could not believe my ears, but he continues on and asks me to attend church with them on Wednesday evening, and I am thinking, *Church, that's the last place I wanna go. No one has fun at church!* I decided I would go but I would dress like I was going out on the town! I had bell-bottom pants on that were silver, gold, black, and white stripes, a snake-skinned shirt open to my belly button, black shoes with white toe-tips, and I was ready for church; you could see me in a dense fog at 500 meters with your parking lights on! No church in their right mind would have me, especially in an Assembly of God church back in the day when long hair, long skirts, no makeup, etc., were the standards. I saw this old man as I approached the church, and he, I assumed, was one of the bouncers; if you don't meet these standards, you have to go! To my surprise, he grabbed my hand and told me that God loved me and he loves me and welcome! That floored me! I went in and sat near my brother and this pastor, who had these coke-bottle glasses on, would point his finger at me under the conviction of the Holy Spirit. I began to weep. I tried hiding the tears by wiping them away, but I could not. I asked my brother Jim if he would come down to the altar with me, he did and I again committed my life to Christ. This time, it began to stick some. I wanted to get into the Bible and read it for myself and I did, but the problem was that the King James Version was for me like reading Mandarin Chinese. I set on trying my darndest to do things the right way. Someone gave me a paraphrased living Bible, and it really made things easier for me to understand. I really did not understand what a personal relationship with God really entailed, but I knew things were going to have to change for me.

Third Tour in Vietnam

I left for Vietnam with my head in my Bible and started reading it as much as possible. When I arrived at the reception station, I was eager to get to my next duty station and start my next tour, but I was not wanting to get myself killed just because I had failed in a few areas of my life, that of being a father and a husband. I just knew because of my newfound faith that my Father God would give me a plush assignment, so when I heard places mentioned, such as Saigon, Cam Rhan Bay, Nha Trang, or other big locations, my name was not called and the anxiety began to rise, then finally I heard "Phillips, Phu Bai," and I asked the Lord to show me where Phu Bai was and it is located twenty to twenty-five miles south of the DMZ (Demilitarized Zone) or the border between North and South Vietnam. Once you get saved, you almost feel invincible, so I gathered my gear and headed for Phu Bai. I was at Phu Bai for about a month or so, and I did not like it one bit, so I did not consult God. I figured I could probably handle a transfer on my own, so I submitted my paperwork and it came back with orders for Camp Eagle which was just seventeen miles south of the DMZ! I did not want to be a missionary to the North Vietnamese Army, so I decided I would consult God the next time I was going to change assignments. One evening, we got mortar fire, and we all went to our designated positions around the camp and hopefully waited for the attack to simmer down, and it did! I was at Camp Eagle for maybe four months, and the 101st was stepping down and preparing to return to the States so they decided to send me to Long Binh where I would be assigned to a logistics unit. I was walking by the chapel and heard some guys singing and playing a guitar so I went in and introduced myself, and they were fired up for Jesus. They asked me if I would join their group and I was not a real good vocalist, but I did play an instrument in middle school and high school so I could keep rhythm and they gave me a tambourine and I joined their group. Our commander was an atheist, and I had to go in and ask him permission to go out to a fire base and share the gospel of Jesus Christ! I entered his office and saluted as normal and told him what I would like to do and he said, "Sure, just fill out a hometown news release."

I think commanders got points or something for allowing their troops to participate in moral activities. We flew out to the fire base that was just hit the night before, and they were running around loading their big guns, and we set up a small makeshift stage and began singing. After we sang, we had to get back on the chopper and head back to base camp. There was so much garbage in my life, I had a hard time forgiving myself, and when you yield to sin, the devil has a nasty way of not letting you forget it! I had my fair share!

Before coming to Vietnam on my third tour, I met a family at this church where I committed my life to Christ and met a big family that had several children in it that all but one was adopted and the mother was Mother of the Year for three or four years running, and their oldest daughter, I think she was eighteen at the time, seemed to be a nice girl and there was some attraction, but I did not want to be distracted at the time. I thought how wonderful it would be if my kids could be in this family while I returned to Vietnam; they would get to know Jesus, and it would be great for them. While I was on leave, I went and picked up my kids from my sister's home in Nebraska and took them to this family in Kent, Washington. I returned to Vietnam, thinking that the kids would adapt and do fine.

The Second Marriage (Disaster)

While in Vietnam, the mother of this family I left my children with said she had a vision from God that I would marry her daughter! She said that if they contacted my children's mother and she signed over her parental rights to me that this was a sign that her daughter and I would marry! The later part of my third tour in Vietnam was uneventful, and I was excited about getting home. It was not long before Barbara and I became more than acquainted and were engaged to get married! I remember being in the church, in a prayer room, and I asked God to specifically tell me yes or no, if I should marry this woman and God answered no! I assumed God had to be mistaken, so I married her. I had orders for Fort Lewis, Washington, and arrived on post with Barbara and my two children. I really did not know Barbara's past. I knew she was adopted into this family and that she was a Korean or Amerasian lady and that she had a rough time in other homes she had been in.

It was not until later in the marriage that some of those homes she was in were pretty traumatic experiences.

Chapter 8

The Cocoa House Ministry and the Chaplaincy

I love the Lord. I just was so immature as a Christian, I was not sure about the relationship thing! I decided that I would ask my commander to allow me to change my MOS one more time, and I went to him and asked him, and he told me that he could not make that decision that a new commander was coming in on Monday and I would have to ask him! The new commander was an infantry officer, and I began to think he will not let me transfer over! I prayed about it, and Monday came and I found myself standing in front of the commander and I saluted and said, "I would like to change my MOS to be a chaplain's assistant."

He said why and I began to share with him how God had touched my life and that I felt I could contribute more to the army and told him about my conversion experience in Vietnam. He leaned back into his chair and lifted his hands and said, "Praise the Lord!"

He was not just the commander of that unit, but he was also the president of the Full Gospel Men's Fellowship in Tacoma, Washington. He said, "Get your paperwork complete, and I will sign it!"

I did, and the next week, I reported to the 593rd Ordnance Group as a chaplain assistant. I did not realize God in the background; the little things He brought about that started me on a course that would change my life forever!

Shortly after my new assignment, God showed me something that kind of took me by surprise. I began to think of dependent military children in the middle school age group, and the Lord said, "How about starting a Cocoa House Ministry?"

There were coffee houses for teenage and young adults but nothing for junior high youth, so the cocoa house, since more young people drank cocoa instead of coffee, seemed like just the right fit! The ministry began to blossom. Barbara and I were involved; we went camping with the youth, and about a year into the marriage, Barbara suggested that my daughter Lisa and son Rick go back to her family and let them spend some time being raised on the farm. They had animals, horses, and the wide outdoors I thought this would be ideal for them, and besides, Barbara was pregnant with our first child, Sarah! We would have three children, Sarah, Sherry, and Suzanne!

The ministry was booming. and we were busy, busy, busy, and I was in debt up to my ears almost. The army overpaid me $5,000, and they began to collect that back, and Barbara had other interests besides me and the kids. I was so busy ministering to other children, my own family was going to hell in a hand basket! I could not see it for the light of day, but eventually, it came to a halt, eight years and three kids and the marriage is over. The army came down with a reclassification order that took me out of the chaplaincy and put me in the infantry. I told the Lord, "If this is what you want, then I want it too," but it was a hard pill to swallow. After about ten months in the infantry, I received a letter from General Bowers informing me to return to the chaplaincy and continue my work there! Unknown to me at the time, the youth from the cocoa house ministry sent a letter to the general and asked that I be placed back into the chaplaincy. I still have those letters today. I received a letter in the mail with two red stars on it, and it was my orders to return to the chaplaincy.

I became the NCOIC of the 3rd Brigade's Chaplain's Office, and one of my assistants was a young man who was more intelligent than I was but had a heart for God, and when you work with people like David Freiheit, they just make you better! David and I competed against other soldiers in our unit for awards.

David was Soldier of the Month.
I was NCO of the Month.

David was Soldier of Quarter.
I was NCO of the Quarter.
David was Soldier of the Year.
And I was NCO of the Year.

Soldiering was my job and I cannot, for the life of me, tell you why the marriage did not work, but I can tell you that I take full responsibility for it not working! I should have never married Barbara in the first place; when God says no, He means just that!

Rick and Lisa stayed at Barbara's parents' home and the three girls stayed with us until I came down on orders for Korea which is a one-year unaccompanied tour. I left for Korea thinking that the children were doing fine.

Chapter 9

Korea

Barbara and I were separated just before I left for Korea and the children, all five of them, stayed at her mother's home. I felt comfortable with that, but inside, I was aching for them. I was assigned to Headquarters 8th Army, the Chaplain's Office, and was asked to report to the 8th Army Chaplain. He asked me if I would like to take a semi-professional assignment to the DMZ. I said I would, and so arrangements were made to assign me to Camp Kittyhawk; on the DMZ, the motto was "In Front of Them All!" I would be the unit's chaplain/chaplain assistant and would provide Bible studies and chapel services for the troops in that unit. I would also have the responsibility of making sure the local orphanage would be helped by the troops and most troops at the end of the month would donate something to the orphanage. I would take the kids down to Yong Song and go to the zoo; they would come and sing every Sunday at our chapel. God impressed on me to write a scripture on the stairs leading up to the chapel, "Psalm 25: Unto thee O Lord do I lift up my soul, Let me not be ashamed and let not my enemies triumph over me" (See photos in middle of book). There were exactly enough words in this scripture to put one on each stair heading up to the chapel. Many people came through Camp Kittyhawk on tours, and they would see that scripture and make a lot of nice remarks about it!

I sent for Barbara in hopes to reconcile our marriage, but it did not seem to take hold. After my tour of duty, I headed home, and my next assignment was Redstone Arsenal, Alabama. Barbara and I tried one last time, but there were just cold embers on the fire. I found out that Barbara was pregnant and gave her an ultimatum: she stays with me and we could try and make it work or she could take the car, return to Washington, and file for divorce. She decided to leave, and of course, I kept the three girls. I had left my children Lisa and Rick at Barbara's mother's home. I had met a girl in a nearby city and we dated awhile, but I had finally come to the conclusion that I did not need to get married; she was too young and already had a child, and it was just not right. I asked God out of desperation to just allow me to raise the kids and do the best I could.

One day at work, at the post chapel, I heard God speak to me about my plans to take the three girls back to Washington and back to Barbara's mother and drop them off and return to Redstone Arsenal, go to school, hang on for two more years, and retire from the army. I was sitting at my desk, and I heard God say to me, "Go," and I made arrangements to travel to Washington. When I arrived at Barbara's mother's home, my son ran out to me and grabbed my leg and said loudly, "Dad, Dad!"

I felt my heart drop some. Lisa was not home yet, but she came in a little later, and I tried to surprise her; she started weeping, and immediately God said, "Take them back with you!"

I had heard from God before and said no. I was not about to let them go this time. I had no idea what I was going to do with five children, but they were mine and my responsibility. Barbara's mother was angry that I was taking my children and even told me I could not take them. I said emphatically, "They are mine, and I am taking them!"

Barbara's mom got into her truck with Rick and Lisa and headed to her pastor's home, and I followed in pursuit. When we arrived, we sat down and discussed what we were going to do with the children, but I knew what God wanted me to do! One of Barbara's other sisters were there and asked if she could talk to me while the pastor took Lisa and Rick to a back room to talk with them. I hesitated about going outside, but something inside of me said, "What could it hurt."

She told me in no uncertain words, "Whatever you do, take the children with you!"

Not knowing anything about the treatment of my kids over the past five or six years, I was intent on taking them; it was a confirmation from God. I went back into the house, and the pastor said, "Rick wants to stay and Lisa wants to go."

I said, "God told me to take them both," and I did. We left the next day.

Barbara had been at a previous home before the one she was living at and her previous adopted mother was very wealthy; she gave me the Mercury she had to transport the kids back, but I sold it without her knowledge and bought bus tickets back to Huntsville. I began my parenting chores. I was not real good at it, but I did the best I could. One Sunday, I surprised Lisa with a Valentine's Day party; she invited a friend, Beth, and they had a great time. Beth's mom came to pick her up, and although Beth's mom looked exceptionally beautiful, I had other fish to fry. Had it not been for the Protestant women of the chapel, I do not know how I would have made it. I had no car and walked to work, after getting the children ready, got my work done, returned home, and started parenting again. I was still in debt and had been for most of military life, but I got a great deal on a car. At church, I had met Beth's mom and we hit it off, but I was exceptionally skeptical because we began to see each other, but this relationship never became physical not like the two previous marriages. Ignorance is no excuse, and even when I thought I was a Christian, my heart had not really been dealt with like it should. I did not understand what 2 Corinthians 5:17 really meant, "Therefore if any man be in Christ he is a new creature, old things are passed away, behold all things become new." You cannot survive in Christianity without reading and studying the Bible, not possible! I knew I had loved Jesus. I just did not let His word sink into my soul and spirit, and therefore, I just kept doing what I thought was the right thing, you know, what Jesus would do!

When Edith and I decided to get married, we went to counseling, something I had never done before. We prayed a lot, and when the temptations became a little fleshy, we would date with all of my kids present; now that's the way to keep the devil at bay! We were married at the Bicentennial Chapel at Redstone Arsenal on February 14, 1983. Our dear friend Richard McAllister sang the song. "Surely the Presence of the Lord Is in This Place" as Edith approached the altar; it was amazing! Now to continue life. My next assignment was to Germany, and we all headed in that direction. It was pretty nice for a while, and as Edie cared for the sheep, I worked like a dog at the office and traveled some on temporary duty. Edie was a Godsend for me and I was always faithful to God and her, and we had a really good marriage. There were times when I had to make some decisions I would rather not want to discuss here, but they were always about the children, not Edie or I; we would not allow our marriage to be destroyed simply because the children misbehaved or they were just being children. I know now that I could have been a much better disciplinarian and came to Edie's rescue and I did at times. Being a strong disciplinarian was one of my weakest areas in raising children.

After four years in Germany, we returned home and retirement. We got quarters off post for a short period of time before we could get a home. I began working as a facility manager (janitor) at a local church, Faith Chapel in Huntsville; it was the church where I had met Edie and we loved the people there! It was rough for Edie and me because the kids were just hard to manage. I have no idea where all the rebellion came from, but I often think of that scripture where it talks about sins of the father visiting their children! Somewhere along the line, I apparently picked up some behaviors my dad had, but I was, at least I thought, a fairly good dad. I was retired and got a letter in the mail asking me if I would come out of retirement and join forces for Desert Storm/Shield! I did and packed my things and the girls stayed with Edie, and I returned to active duty at Dover Air Force Base as a senior chaplain assistant with duty at the post mortuary. I was there only a week before the war started to slow down and was asked to take on an assignment at Fort Leonardwood, Missouri. I did and had my family join me.

Edie and the girls arrived, but Sarah just took off and we had no idea where she was, and Edie was extremely upset that I did not go and find her. She was seventeen going on eighteen, and I had no idea where she was. This had upset Edie so much that she took a plane back home; she left me! After my short tour there, the girls and I traveled back to Alabama. Edie thought for sure I was going to leave her, divorce her, but I reassured her I was not allowing that to happen; after all, we believed that God put us together and no one was going to separate us, not even the kids. Sarah called me one day and told me she had a job! I said, "What are you doing?"

And she told me she was working in a carnival! Eventually, Sarah and Sherry and even Suzanne all headed back to their mother's home in Washington. There was a lot of heartache there, even with Edith, and we simply prayed about our girls and told the Lord, "We surrender these girls to you, they are yours, please watch over them!"

I decided to go back to Faith Chapel full time and attend college! I had one college course while I was at Fort Lewis where I got my high school diploma. I was so scared because I could only read on a second grade level. The teacher gave us an assignment, "Write down something you are familiar with on an 8×10 sheet of blank paper, bring it in the next day, and we will go from there!"

I wrote down love, agape, philios, and eros! We returned to class. I thought I could cover the types of love, and I prepared to do that. The teacher told us to fold the papers in half, bring them to the front of the class, and place them all on the table! Oh! Oh! I did and returned to my desk. He then instructed us, after he shuffled the papers around, to come up and pick a paper and discuss it! I was the seventh in line and just happened to pick up my paper on love, and I began to see how God moves in people's lives in a miraculous way! I got an A in this class, my first A ever in school. I continued my education, and after five and a half years, I got my degree in, would you believe, education! I would be a secondary educator, and I was totally excited; the girls were with their mom, and Edie and I were by ourselves, but we had some really wonderful and awesome grandchildren from Edie's side of the family that we would enjoy for years to come! I applied for the military instructor at Madison County High School in Gurley, Alabama. I was replacing a sergeant major! For three years, I had to travel about fifteen to twenty miles to school, and after coaching in different sports, I had to travel back home until a new principal asked me if I would be interested in teaching at Hazel Green Middle School, approximately four blocks from my home. He was in need of a basketball coach, and I wanted to get closer to home. A new school opened up in Meridianville, Alabama, and I took the job. Upon my interview with the principal, Terry Davis, he asked me what makes me think I would be a good teacher for eighth grade students, and when I replied that "I had three years of combat experience," he said, "You're hired!"

Chapter 10

Education

Since my three older brothers had already made their mark at school when I arrived, the teachers thought I was one of them! I had a very hard time with math, and reading was the worst of all my subjects to grasp. Middle school was not much better, and I spent two years in the sixth grade, and I guess they decided that they needed to push me on so I do not take up permanent residence at the elementary school. Middle school was another waste of time for me. I just had no interest in English, math, social studies, or anything else. Art was my favorite subject along with band! I did not get interested in sports until high school.

I played a trombone in the high school band and loved marching! I also ran track, and one day, my friends hassled me about playing football. I went out for the team and made first string. My mom passed away during spring practice, and that was the end of my football career! I played flag and tackle football in the army on unit teams and played four years of softball. In softball, out of 174 games, we only lost four; we were really good.

Chapter 11

She Is Dead, Daddy, She Is Dead!

It was a usual day, and I was heading for work at Madison County High School. I normally went by Buckhorn High School where my supervisor was and checked in with them to see if there were any special instructions for the day. As I entered his office, there was a phone call for me on my cell phone. I asked to be excused because the call was from my daughter, Sarah, in Washington State. When I called back, there was this hysterical voice on the other end of the line repeating the phase, "She is dead, Daddy, she is dead!"

Suzie was dead, and as Sarah and I talked, the medics were administering a procedure called pericardiocentesis, where they place a needle in her heart to try and remove excess fluid around it. Come to find out Suzie has just had a baby a few weeks earlier and had to use the restroom; she laid little Maurice down on a rug on the floor and then collapsed herself. No one knows the pain of losing a child except the parent that loses that child. Suzie was the last to leave the house, and we had hoped she would stay and that she would make decisions that would have made life better for her. She met a young man and apparently fell in love with him, and he later was arrested and put in jail for fifteen years for armed robbery. I might add that he is out of prison and doing very well, and he is the father of my grandson and I love him!

I had the privilege of sharing at her funeral and told the guys and gals that were there that if they ever wanted to see Suzie again, maybe they should consider giving their lives to Christ since I believe Suzie loved the Lord but, much like her dad, did not always make the right decisions about relationships in life. Suzie was always joyful, just filled with enthusiasm, and she, along with her sister, Sherry attended Spiritual Warfare Camp, a Christian camp that I had been introduced to in 1989. When Edith and I prayed after the girls left that we were putting them in God's hands as well as Lisa and Rick, we actually felt a peace flow over us and found the only way, we believe, that we could have successfully dealt with this tragedy.

Chapter 12

Spiritual Warfare Camp

My daughters, Suzie and Sherry, were asked to go to a camp known as Spiritual Warfare Camp. I was working at Faith Chapel at the time, and being a soldier for nearly twenty-seven years and being a part of youth ministries for nearly twenty of those years, I thought this would be really good for them!

Spiritual Warfare Camp was based on military training and discipline, a sort of spiritual boot camp. It was around 1992 or 1993 that I was on my way to pick the girls up and decided to go a few hours early and check this camp out! While I was there, I saw them doing push-ups and running and being chewed out by some drill sergeants and I thought, *This is just right up my alley.* I had been involved with youth ministries a lot, and when I started college, I had planned to go into psychology, but then after my first semester, I changed my mind and headed into education; being a teacher sounded so much more fun to me than psychology.

The general at the camp, Louie Barnett, was actually a Vietnam veteran, a Marine who received the Purple Heart; he was actually a corporal in the Marines, but at Warfare Camp, he was the general. I asked if I could be a part of the ministry as the sergeant major; although I was a retired sergeant first class, I was a SGM at Warfare

Camp. It was a powerful camp for young people. The motto of the camp was:

> I believe that I have been called to be a soldier
> Of Jesus Christ and I am engaged in continuous
>   warfare
> With Satan and his host. Therefore, my life must
>   reflect
> The personal disciplines of a soldier while here
>   in this
> Present world.

One of the responsibilities of each soldier or cadet was to memorize this motto and hide it in their heart!

There were six days of camp from arriving and checking in to graduation. I could mention several young men and women who have gone to warfare camp and have become pastors; my grandson Joshua is presently pastoring a local church here in Huntsville. I like to believe that Warfare Camp had an impact on his life. There are young people who have stepped into almost every area of ministry including missionary work to different parts of the world!

Making Memories at Warfare Camp

Day 1, Week 1: Registration, normally the cadets are asked to get off the buses by two very professional retired military people known as drill sergeants. They get in the kids' faces, and there are no hands-on stuff; they just chew and rechew, like a cow and its cud, to help mold young people to do the things they believe God wants them to do. It is the beginning of boot camp for them, and if you have ever been to boot camp without the profanity, of course, then you have some idea of what that is like. Of all the years that we have had warfare camp, I know of only one kid, from Mississippi, that returned home before camp started. Below are listed some emotional moments, moments of laughter and moments of serious spiritual growth.

1. When my daughter Suzie passed away, one of the women counselors or drill sergeants shared with me that even though I had lost Suzie, there were hundreds of girls that have been my daughters over the years at Warfare Camp. Once we established the fact that all the young ladies who attended camp were the sergeant major's daughter and that the emphasis at camp was developing a relationship with God, not some male camper, things began to change for the boys who thought they could cuddle up to the SGM daughters...not so!

There was this time at camp when I gave a part of the introduction to camp at the in-processing briefing of all the cadets and told them that if any of the guys had an interest in my daughters, they would have to see me first to get my approval (which never happened anyway); our focus was to be on Christ and how Christ would change our hearts and minds to follow after Him! This one guy thought he did not have to follow the guidelines at camp and, during the briefing, sat too close to one of the SGM's daughters. I addressed him after the briefing and told him that he needed to stay at least six feet away from any girl at camp. I figured that was plenty of room for them to hear each other. I dropped them for ten push-ups and we continued with camp business. That afternoon, it was Commander's Time (that would be another term for free time, if you were a civilian)! I noticed that they were walking together down this hill heading for the beach on the lake and a swimming pool! I stopped them and asked them why they decided to walk closer than I had instructed them earlier. They hemmed and hawed and I told them, in a firm voice, to drop (drop is a term used in airborne training, meaning get down in the push-up position) and give me ten push-ups. It was a type of discipline, and it worked! I got them up and told them they could continue their voyage down to the lake, but he would have to walk on one side of the road and she would have to walk on the other! I gave them a few minutes and thought, *I know the flesh very well.* I went back to the assembly hall, picked up my megaphone, and headed to the lake! Lo and behold, guess who was out in a paddle boat together! There were several people on the beach and at the pool, and I blasted away on the megaphone and told him, "Hey, you little low-life gutter ball, you bring my daughter back here right now."

Dressed in my battle dress uniform with drill sergeant hat and all, they turned around and headed to the dock where I met them and dropped them for push-ups. I chewed her out first lovingly and gently and then told the boy to stay in the push-up position until gravity took over! After I had chewed him out and sent him back up to the assembly area, I was walking away when some woman, a mother, came up to me and asked me, "Do you make house calls?"

Prior to camp, the year my daughter Suzie passed away, I had to make an errand to the store and my five-year-old grandson, Cameron, was in the car with me. I was of course somewhat distraught over her death, and as I sat in the car, I gently pounded on the stirring wheel and said, "God, what do you want me to do? What do you want me to do?"

And Cameron looked over at me and said, "I know what God wants you to do," and somewhat shocked, I said, "What does God want me to do?"

He said to me, in that innocent little voice, "God wants you to fasten my seatbelt!"

It seemed as if the burden had lifted, and now we could get on with life! Out of the mouth of babes!

2. A drill sergeant and I were walking past a girl's cabin when we heard some screaming and yelling, and we of course stopped in to see what was happening. The girls thought they had seen a mouse and were jumping off their bunks, out the doors, and panic ensured! We, however, came to their rescue! The drill sergeant pretended that he found the mouse and went after the girls with cupped hands; of course, there was no mouse in his hands, but they didn't

know it! An idea came to me, and later that morning, when one of the local stores opened, I went down and picked up a toy mouse that cats usually play with and a can of cream of mushroom soup and a can of vegetable beef soup! We told the girls we would have lunch with them, and as we sat down to eat, the drill sergeant cupped his hands over his mouth with the toy mouse's tail handing out of his hands.

I said, "Drill Sergeant, you don't look very well," and he gets up and runs into the doorway just a few feet away from the table and begins to make sounds as if he is throwing up! He dips the cream of mushroom soup and the vegetable soup in a tray and drops the toy mouse in the soups! He returns to the table, sits down, and the girls watch carefully as other cadre come over, and we all dip into the tray, getting the biggest piece of meat we can find, and there the mouse sits with its tail hanging over the tray and they asked me, "SGM, do we have to eat lunch?" and my reply was, "At warfare camp there are three requirements, you eat, sleep and exercise."

They reluctantly went back to eating, very slowly I might add! Twenty years later, they still remember that moment and laugh about it!

3. One year at camp, my grandson shows up with my grand-daughter, and he was wearing pretty earrings! He had been testing the waters at home, and so I suggested to another drill sergeant to go over and dress him down about the earrings. We normally do not wear earrings in the military, and since camp was based on a military model, we had to make sure everyone complied. The drill sergeant goes over and says, "Hey, boy," in his Southern tongue, "those are real pretty earrings you have on and you know what, I have a dress that will match those earrings just fine. If you don't remove those pretty things from your ears, I will put that dress on you tonight at dinner!"

Josh immediately removes his earrings, and the look on his face was precious! Before the end of camp, I was given the honor of baptizing Josh, and he is now an associate pastor of a local church in our area. It is hard to express the joy of seeing anyone making such a decision but to follow through in ministry is more than just frosting on the cake! There are hundreds of stories I can tell of young men and women who have committed themselves in ministry all over the world who have been to warfare camp. It's amazing!

4. I have been privileged to attend camp in Michigan, Alabama, Mississippi, North Carolina, and Tennessee. One year in North Carolina during an outdoor activity, a confidence course, there was a squad of boys who were unusually rude, and we usually find some type of special blessing that might get their attention back to the mission of warfare camp. Camp is not the place for you to do your thing; we are trying to encourage young men and women to take their relationship with Christ seriously, and it usually demands warfare, spiritual warfare! At midnight, we got the boys up and took them down to the dock; we showed them how to jump out of an airplane (it's an airborne thing)! They, one by one jumped off the dock into the water, then we rolled them in the sand, making sugar cookies out of them and then chewed them out, told them what we expected of them in camp, and would not tolerate any more of their foolishness while at camp! About 3:00 a.m., this same squad came back to our quarters and woke us up, washed out feet, we prayed with them, and the rest of the week was amazing as in just a few short moments, these young men learned a valuable lesson is life!

5. Another incident happed in North Carolina, but it had to do with a kid who was hired as staff by the camp and worked in the dining facility; he was not a member of our group, but he had an interest in one of the sergeant major's daughters. The young lady came to me and said that this guy was asking some personal questions, and I told her, "Do not answer his questions. I will deal with this!"

I went to the camp director and told him that I did not want this guy making any passes at my daughters, and I would appreciate it if he would stop! We agreed! Well, this young fella pushed the wrong button when he later, after graduation, asked my daughter for her phone number; she came to me and I said, "Well, let's give to him."

I wrote down my number and told the girl to tell him she was eager to hear from him. About a week later, I get this call from this guy and said, "Are you that low-life gutter ball who try to get next to my daughter at camp?"

Suddenly the phone went silent! I believe he got the message!

6. I created a sergeant major's Hooah! Hooah! card. On the front it says, "Seeking sympathy, compassion, and mercy! See the sergeant major!" On the card are several Bible verses, and when one of the young cadets thinks he has a better idea than God, I share the scripture on the card and punch the card. For example, let's say the cadet is feeling bad because he/she did not get a letter from home that day. I would take his card and show the scripture relating to his perceived problem! 2 Corinthians 3:3 says, "You show that you are a letter from Christ, the result of our ministry, written not with ink but with the Spirit of the living God, not on tablets of stone but on tablets of human hearts." After reading the scripture, we would pray and she or he could continue through the day. We take Satan seriously because he is the enemy and he does not care about anything except taking your soul to hell with him. We want our young people to learn how to fight the enemy, and that's exactly what he is, but he is a defeated foe as witnessed at Calvary through the shed blood of Jesus Christ. It is hard for some adults to grasp this, let alone young people. That is where faith comes in!

7. When the cadets first come to camp, we have them in a formation and are chewing them out for no reason at all; well, actually we have a reason! The enemy, Satan, says he comes

to kill, steal, and destroy and he does not care who gets hurt in the battle (John 10:10). So we play the devil's advocate and teach our young people how to win the battles they face every day in their lives. We asked a young couple, parents of a cadet, if they would like to partake in a little fun thing with their child. We had the parents near the front of the formation, and we were confronting their son and we said to him, "Tim. Come here, are your parents here?"

"Yes, sir," he said.

I dropped him for ten push-ups because you only call officers "Sir," you call enlisted men and women by their respective ranks, for example, sergeant, drill sergeant, or sergeant major, etc. We said to him, "Point out your parents."

"They are over there."

We yelled to the parents, "Hey! Is this your offspring?"

They said yes, and we told the parents to drop! Tim's eyes about fell out of his head; he thought we were going after his momma and daddy; we had a great laugh later and created another memory for their family! At no time do we ever belittle a child, but we do have our methods of getting our point across.

8. Some well-intentioned guests at the campsite thought we were harassing the cadets and called the police. We greeted the police and gave them a briefing about the camp, what we taught, the discipline we used, and after that exercise was over, the officers wanted to know when they could sign their kids up for Warfare Camp!

9. One morning during PT (physical training), we had just completed a one-mile run and it had been raining. A young cadet had a ranger patch on his uniform, and I asked him, "Did you earn that patch?"

His response was no but that the shirt had belonged to a relative. I said, "If you did not earn it, you should not be wearing it," and I got closer to him, rose up on my toes, and gripped the patch with my teeth and ripped it off his shirt! His eyes bulged from their sockets, and during the entire week, I am not sure if he kept his eyes off me.

At Warfare Camp, we emphasize the fact that Satan is not greater than you or any other saint; we need to know how to dress for battle (Ephesians 4:13–18). Every young person who comes to camp comes with some baggage that they either are not familiar with or they just do not know how to deal with it, and it is our duty to help them navigate through the tough issues of life. It is only through troubles and problems that we can actually grow in Christ. It is a huge issue when you are told to love your enemies and do good to those who persecute you, especially in these trying days. Problems promote spiritual maturity, and that is what Warfare Camp has been about the last thirty-five years that I have been blessed to be a part of that unique ministry.

This book was written as a gift to my children, grandchildren, and great-grandchildren to let them see what their Dad, Opa, and Great-Granddad has suffered through in hopes they will make the right choice early in life. I have chased the world and found nothing of value, but when Christ came to me and he had to make the trip more than once because I was either too stubborn, too stupid, or too self-centered to take Him at His word when we met initially, for real, in elementary school, again in Vietnam, and again at Redstone Arsenal, Alabama. Finally, He got through to me, and it was then that I surrendered to Him.

It is difficult to fathom His love for me after I had screwed up so many times in my life, but God died for me and His love is beyond comprehension, and that's why you have to institute your faith and allow His Holy Spirit to come into your life and to take up residency.

Photo of SFC Henry M. Phillips at retirement
in 1989 Redstone Arsenal, Alabama.

Specialist 4th class David Freiheit and Specialist 6th
Class Henry M. Phillips receiving awards for solder
and NCO of the month, quarter and year, 3rd Brigade,
9th Infantry Division, Fort Lewis, Washington.

Retired U.S. Army veteran Henry Phillips is ready
for Spiritual Warfare Camp July 23–28th 2007.

Sitting on the stairs leading to the Chapel at Camp Kitty
Hawk, South Korea, our motto "In Front of the All"

Burial of my Daughter Suzanne Bethel Phillips—
she was awesome in every sense of the word.

Preparing to welcome young cadets to Spiritual
Warfare Camp, Welcome my little pretties!

This is my Baptist in Nha Trang, South Vietnam with
Christian Missionary Alliance missionaries, Lem and
Marge Morgan. My greatest life event. 1968

Spiritual Warfare Graduation, two of the most outstanding young
ladies you will ever want to meet. Heather and Huntre Basnight.

Inside the Camp Kitty Hawk Chapel, preparing
for service, DMZ South Korea.

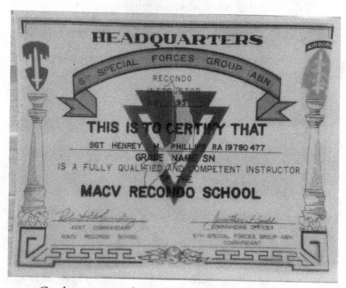

Graduation certificate from the MACV Recondo
Schhool in South Vietnam, one of the most
challenging military schools I ever attended.

Two soldiers stationed on the DMZ
guarding the Bridge of No return.

One of the most exciting things for the young orphans
was a trip to the zoo in Seoul, South Korea. Soldiers
and orphans alike enjoyed it immensely.

The Paul Bunya incident caused the lives of North Koreans and a few American soldiers; one Korean and one U.S. soldier stand guard near the bridge of no return which is just meters from this tree.

The Cadre room where guards could relax, and chat hangs the hats of those men who were stationed in the DMZ for a year and as tribute to their service their hats were hung on the wall. My hat is at the far left the one with the cross.

This is the chapel where I was stationed at Camp Kitty Hawk! My place of business. On the stairs is stenciled the words "I Trust In You; Lord, Let Me Not Be Ashamed And Let Not My Enemies Triumph Over Me" [Psalm 25:2] As far as I know it is still there today!

The Meridianville Middle School Drill Team and Color
Guard performing at the annual Special Olympics in
Huntsville, Alabama. They were exceptionally great.

One of many Spiritual Warfare Camp drill teams and color guard
that performed extremely well. Each year a new crop of youth
would volunteer and each year they performed exceptionally well.

The Meridianville Middle School Color Guard presenting the
Colors at a special recognition program for students. One of
these students is presently a captain in the United States Army.

Spiritual Warfare Camp poster is raised to
welcome new recruits to camp.

Spiritual Warfare Camp Color Guard and Drill Team.
Every year new recruits who probably never marched
before camp preformed in an outstanding manner. We
have had warfare camp primarily in Michigan, then in
Alabama, Tennessee, Mississippi, and North Carolina.

Chapter 13

Teaching and Coaching

After retiring from the military and graduating from college, the field of education had really settled in for me. Never taught school, and if the teachers that taught me could see what has happened to me, they would probably turn over in their graves.

Real teaching for me started at Meridianville Middle School in Meridianville, Alabama. It was always my belief that if you are going to teach any students, you have to first genuinely love them, and if you do, then teaching will be fun, exciting, and my experience has been that most students learn very well under a warm and loving environment.

Below are a series of incidents that happened in my class and which excited my students to feel more comfortable learning:

1.) It was my first day of teaching seventh graders world history, but I struggled to draw their attention and then this thought came to mind. I took an Alka Seltzer tablet and put it in my mouth, and as I began to foam at the mouth, my students were mesmerized. They gathered around me to see if there was anything they could do. After forty seconds or so, I recovered and wiped the foam from my mouth. They began to ask me what was wrong with me! I told them that it might be a Vietnam flashback. It was time for lunch and during the lunch, one young student came up to me and asked me if I could have another flashback since he apparently enjoyed the first one so much. I told him that it could happen at any moment for the next three to four weeks. They were sitting on the edge of their seat, anticipating another flashback, but it opened the door for the opportunity to reach their minds and, I suspect, a few hearts.

2.) Placed on each window in my upstairs classroom were the signs that read, "GIRLS EXIT" and on the window "BOYS EXIT, please don't be alarmed it was only a thirty-five-foot drop." Fortunately, we never had to use those exits but the thought was nice on occasions.

3.) There were times during the latter part of the year when I would have the students prepare games similar to Monopoly. There were three to four students in a group, and they had to meet certain requirements and had to participate in the projects, or their grade would be reflective of how much they participated. We would use three chapters of a book, and one of the students in the group would have to come up with a title for the game; another student would work on cards with questions on one side and answers on the other. Students would begin work on the poster-board-sized game. Finally one student would have to come up with the rules, but all students in the game would have to come up with ten different questions plus game pieces used in the game and no commercial gameboard pieces were allowed. After completion of the games, a test would be administered from the question from each student's gameboards. We would meet in the library and the principal. Finally the principal would reward the first-place winners with $50.00, second place $25.00, and third place $10.00. The funds for these games came from my pocket and sometimes teachers just have to give up a little something for their students to learn a few things.

4.) Sometimes I would give nicknames to my students and one particular student had the last name of "Keil," pronounced kill, so I gave her the name Road Kill and she did not seem to mind it, but the following Monday, her mom made a visit to my classroom and was somewhat angry and told me she did not think her daughter wanted to be called Road Kill, so after the apology, she left and we were fine. On Wednesday of that week, she returned and said it would be okay to call her daughter Road Kill. It seems that she was getting a lot of attention, all fun of course, and from that moment on things were fine. This young lady has three beautiful children and is the wife of a youth pastor and is one of the finest young women I know and am privileged to know.

5.) Here are a few comments that students that I have had the privilege of teaching made recently. Usually when one of my past students see me at Walmart or Costco or out and about, he/she comes up to me and says, "Are you Mr. Phillips?" My first response is "Are you filing charges?" I cannot count the number of undisciplined students I have had on one hand.

(a) Justin Calaway: Justin is a captain in the United States Army and was a member of our school color guard and also a student in my class.

He writes:

I want to thank you for your inspiration, dedicated leadership, and service because I likely would not have chosen this path if it weren't for your mentoring during my time at school. I am so grateful to have had you as a teacher and coach so early in life, and I honestly can't thank you enough.

—Justin Calaway
Captain, United States Army

(b) Justin Riddle is a nurse and was an exceptional baseball player and shares this:

> Coach Phillips if the perfect example of leadership. Humility of his own personal convictions makes him a great mentor on life. Always living a sacrificial life, as evident by serving his country and unconditionally loving his wife, unwittingly makes Coach an example to live by for everyone in our community. Whether in the classroom or on the field, Coach devoted his life to molding the minds of children. His steadfast faith in Christ is the most important thing we can learn from him.

—Mr. Justin Riddle
Nurse

(c) Rachael Holaway has a business major and has this to say about Coach Phillips:

> Mr. Phillips was my seventh-grade history teacher and he certainly left a lasting impression. He made a potentially dull subject fun by pitting the girls against the boys in "SAT wars" as a way to review the material. It's been twenty years, but I have never forgotten Mr. Phillips saying that as far as he was concerned, the Bible was history, so he'd teach it if he wanted to. I've encountered Mr. Phillips many times in the years since he was my teacher and he always has a kind word to say. He even took the time to pray with me about a job after a long period of unemployment. I feel very blessed to have had Mr. Phillips as a teacher.

—Rachael Holaway
Businesswoman

(d) Coach Phillips was my teacher and one of my football coaches while I was in eighth grade at Meridianville Middle School. I always looked forward to having Coach Phillips as my teacher. Coach Phillips was very well-known at Meridianville and everyone wanted to be in his class. Coach Phillips was always incredibly positive and upbeat. You never knew if anything ever affected him outside of class. He seemed to always be happy. As a teacher that attitude translated very well to the students. I remember all of his students being very interactive during class. Coach always made something as boring as history fun and exciting. Coach played a lot of games that were challenging and fun but allowed for us to remember what we were learning. Coach has made an impression on my life from the first day I met him. This has now been over fifteen years ago. I have had the honor to know Coach Phillips outside the classroom through church. Since I have grown into adult life, we have developed a friendship that includes weekly Bible studies in our men's accountability group. I genuinely enjoy the wisdom that Coach is able to share with us through his many life experiences. I will always remember and cherish all the time spent with this wonderful man of God. It is truly an honor and pleasure to have been one of many lives that he has influenced.

"Don't spit in the wind" (Coach Philips)

—Cameron Norton
Modeling and Simulation Engineer

(e) Coach Phillips was my history teacher in middle school. There was never a dull moment in his class. You never knew what he was going to do or when he was going to yell out when it was quiet you hear a pin drop just to scare us or get our attention. Ha! Ha! Rarely did he give homework and when he did, it was usually just an assignment we didn't finish in class. He really cared about his students, and it showed that he wanted us all to learn and was very patient with us if we didn't understand something. Little did I know that he would become family several years later. I'm very thankful that God laced him in my grandmother's life. He has been incredibly good to her and for that I will forever be thankful.

—Mrs. Haley Whaley
Businesswoman/Owner

(f) As a middle-school girl in the eighth grade, I had heard stories of Coach Phillips and his history class. I was super excited but quite nervous the first day of school. I knew he would see my last name and make the connection. Coach Phillips was a football coach and would know we were related as he saw my last name, and he did make the connection. Coach Phillips was a football coach, and he knew when he saw my last name. My brother, Alan, and I have quite different personalities. Alan could make friends and talk to anyone, but I was very shy when it came to meeting someone for the first time. I will never forget Coach Phillips calling roll and reaching my name, "Rachael...um... you must be Ski's sis!" he said.

"Yes, that's me," I replied. Coach just chuckled and kept calling roll. From that day on, that was the favorite history class I ever took. I left that class with a few nicknames. One of my favorites was "Rachel Alphabet" (my last name was a doozy). I remember Coach was always cracking jokes in his class and even thought I was pretty shy, and his jokes somehow eased my timidity and brought me a little more out of my shell. His class was by far my favorite eighth-grade class. I looked forward to it every day! It was probably my favorite because he was so passionate about what he taught, and this passion made the information stick in your brain like glue. He had fought in the Vietnam War for the US Army to defend our country and now he was pouring his knowledge and experiences into the younger generation. He knew that we would be the future generations to come. He taught us with great excitement and enthusiasm. You could not take a nap in his class. Looking back, I realized that there are only a handful of teachers that I remember being so motivated to teach us and who actually cared. Coach was one of those teachers. I was blessed to be in his class, and I know that my classmates would say the same! Now that I am an adult with a family of my own, Coach is still a great leader in my life. I am not sure when he started coming to church, but I'll never forget his passion for spiritual warfare camp. His passion about teaching world history spilled over into a passion to serve Christ and speak life into teenagers that so desperately needed a touch from God. He still serves in our church to this day. He is the perfect example of a servant. He served our country for our freedoms. He served me and so many other students, teaching us about his personal experiences and the experiences of other soldiers. He served in my church, continuing to speak truth and life into young persons who desperately needed it. Now he serves in my church as part of the men's ministry and is active in our senior adult ministry also. It has been a blessing and continues to be a blessing getting to be a younger generation under the leadership like Coach's.

—Rachael Ostrzycki Norton
Dialysis Specialist

Constitutional Bingo was a game I created and sold to Teacher's Discovery for a few bucks. I tried to help kids not just learn but to enjoy the process because a happy mind is a mind that will learn.

In 2001 Mr. Phillips was nominated and won the Teacher of the Year Award for Middle Schools in Madison County. It was one of my highlights of my career, but thanks go to so many others who were part of this distinguished award. The Bible verse that I have hung onto since my commitment to Christ is Proverbs 27:2: "Let someone else praise you, and not your own mouth; an outsider, not your own lips."

At Meridianville Middle School, I was asked to coach football. I had some experience but I was never a head coach, never called plays, never ran the game, but my job was to instill in these young men how important it was to push yourself where you never pushed yourself before. Since I had spent twenty-seven years in the military and in Vietnam with Special Forces, I knew what it was like to push yourself. The RECONDO School in Vietnam was the most challenging of all the tactical schools I have ever attended and not realizing that days in RECONDO would prepare me to participate these young men's lives.

There was a player who weighed close to 320 lbs. and for an eighth grader that is a lot of weight to haul around, but this young man pushed himself in the seventh grade and continued to push himself in the eighth grade. When he arrived in high school, he was one of the dominant players on the high school team.

I remember in practice one day when it was hot and dusty, and if the players were sluggish, I would send them down to a small creek just 350 yards from the practice field at that time and they were to pick up a rock and return it to me and it was to be wet when they got back. They all began running down to the small creek, and when they returned, you see their helmets bobbing in the dust looking like one of those warrior films like *The 300*. It was especially impressive that year we bought home one of the two county championships for our school. We had coaches that were believers and we prayed before and sometimes after practices. It is an absolute joy to install godly principles in the lives of young people.

The principal asked me to coach soccer. I knew nothing about soccer, and I didn't even know the ball was round. The principal could not get any other teacher to coach, and many kids wanted to play, so I solved this problem by allowing some parents who had played the game and were really good at it to coach and I would act as the CEO and let them work with the kids. Our records were not all that great, but the kids enjoyed the game, and although our record was not too great, we did play a team that was probably the best in the county who had a coach from the Caribbean Islands and he was great. Their team had won all their games by ten or nine points. They crushed everyone, however. When we played them, they only beat us by three. I might add that five minutes into the game, it was called because of rain but we still held the best record against them even though it was a loss.

Earlier when I first started teaching, my first assignment was at Madison County High School in Gurley, Alabama, and it was challenging, exciting, and filled with hope. I was clear to me that this was what I wanted to do for the rest of my life!

My first assignment was the Army JROTC program (Junior Reserved Officers Corps). This involved teaching young men and women how they could advance their careers in the military, preferably the United States Army! Oftentimes teachers are asked to coach if their schedules permit, and for me it was a great opportunity to learn some new skills for myself. The sports that I had been offered to coach were football, baseball, and softball of which I had taken the greatest interest in football. The JROTC program was struggling and so my job was a tough one. Some students, not all, were special needs students which none would be admitted into the army because of these disabilities but we took them anyway.

One morning I was in my classroom and one of my students collapsed; she died later from a heart issue. It is always hard when someone you know and have taught had lost their life. We recovered but that is not always easy. We developed a drill team and color guard, and it was exceptionally good. What I have learned in teaching and coaching is that we can accomplish anything as a group of dedicated young men and women if we just simply work together and appreciate one another. There would be no mountain too high to climb, no sea too big to sail, and no limit to what we can learn and pass on to others. I learn so much from these young people and have always believed that if you move on and have learned little from those you teach, it is a tragedy.

Andrew Garrison
Owner, Garrison Outdoor Solutions
(Excavation and Hauling)

Coach Phillips was my seventh- and eighth-grade history teacher at Bethlehem Christian Academy from 2013 to 2015, and his class was unforgettable. He created a hands-on learning experience that I will always remember. He is a "been there done that" kind of guy, which not only makes him a great teacher but also a great mentor to anyone around him. One of my best memories of Coach was when I was in the eighth grade. Every morning, a few friends of mine and I would get to school early so we could play basketball before class, and Coach caught up to what we were doing, and he started getting there early as well to shoot some hoops with us, and that meant more to us than he could have imagined.

Ashley (West) Elmore

My name is Ashley (West) Elmore, and I was in Henry's seventh-grade history class at Hazel Green Middle School in 1998. Of course, back then, we all called him Coach Phillips. The thing I remember most about Coach is how joyful he always was. He truly loved his kids, and that love shined through every day. History class can be dull, but it never was that way in his class from all of the stories about his military days to making a history-inspired board game, he tried his hardest to make his students love all things history. He wasn't just concerned about his students inside the classroom walls. I played many sports at Hazel Green, and Coach always knew how we were doing and was one of our biggest fans. And it wasn't just sports, from being a part of the FCA (Fellowship of Christian Athletes) to JROTC, he cared about students with all different interests. And what none of us knew is that as invested and involved as he was in students' lives, he was also a dedicated and devoted husband who was caretaker for his wife in declining health, as well as a committed member of his church. I truly did not know how he did it all.

In 2007, I met my husband, and he ended up being Henry's step grandson! (The impacts that Henry has had on my husband's life are just too numerous to list here. That's a whole story in itself.) So these days, he isn't just coach to me and my family, he was the best man at my wedding and is opa to my children. His favorite joke about us is that he knows that he must have been a good teacher when his students start following him home! The sacrificial love and service that he lives out shines through in every aspect of his life. And I pray that my son, Henry, will represent Christ in the same way his namesake has throughout his life.

Lon Ostrzycki
Pastor of North Lindsey Lane Baptist Church

From my very first day at the new middle school, Coach Henry Phillips has always left a remarkable impression on me. Whether it was his booming voice through the halls or his infectious humor on the football field, Coach Phillips's influence always left an impact on students and players alike. There is so much that I can say about his unconventional style, sage wisdom, and his life stories, but perhaps the most significant thing to me is how he transcended school activities and became a great friend and mentor to my life. I consider myself blessed to have had the privilege to have him pour into my life.

Conclusion

I am going to share some fun things that took place with my family over the years that might bring a smile to your face:

1. During the wedding rehearsal of my third wife, Edith, our children were seated in the pews in the chapel. All the pews had kneelers since other denominations, besides Protestants, used the facility or chapel. My daughter Sherry pulled a kneeler down, and my son Rick said, "Those are for Catholics."

    Sherry said, "I know, we are Catholics!"

    My other daughter Sarah said, "No, we aren't, we're prostitutes!"

    She meant Protestants.

    My wife, Edie, her mom, and I were driving home from a sweetheart banquet. Edie says, "Would you like to go parking?"

    I said, "Momsie can be our chaperone!"

    Momsie replied, "Do you all know an old man who could go with us?"

2. Sherry gave Dad a green wallet that he was given two years ago from Edie for his birthday. Dad had given it to Sarah, who gave it to Sherry, who gave it back to Dad! Happy birthday, Dad!

3. Adam, our grandson, added this classic funny saying to our collection while staying with us before joining his dad overseas. He told us that God only cussed one time in the Bible. When told God never cussed in the Bible, he informed us that Jesus cussed a fig tree and it died!

Through my entire life, God has been present, but I have not always been attentive. Like many others who have sinned and sinned again, God still stands ready to rescue us from ourselves and deliver us from the snares of sin. If you can imagine continuously rejecting God by poor behavior, ignoring His comforting Holy Spirit, the guilt begins to rise and you distance yourself because of your shame—at least I did. But then one day, when I, like the prodigal son, came to my senses and turned away from sin and decided to commit my life to His service and to follow after His word, life changed wonderfully for me!

I still struggle with debt but will soon be free, with bad days and not thinking through issues, but my God is so concerned with me and His love is so awesome and deep, it is sometimes hard for me to fathom, but He does love me, and for that, I am grateful and trust Him daily for not just my needs but getting me through each day and teaching, as a loving Father does, to deal with issues in my life like His son Jesus did!

About the Author

Henry Phillips (Coach) is a high school dropout, joined the U.S. Army in 1963, spent 3 years in Vietnam, 1 year in Korea on the DMZ and was called back to active duty after retirement for Desert Storm/Shield. He graduated from Athens State College in 1994 with a degree in education and started teaching in High school and middle schools in Madison County Alabama. He has coached football, baseball, softball and soccer and also directed the only middle school drill team in the state. He was teacher of the year in 2001 and runner up for Christian Educator of the Year in 2002–2003. He has been involved in Youth Ministry for more than 35 years. He is presently retired and in remission from Multiple Melanoma.

CPSIA information can be obtained
at www.ICGtesting.com
Printed in the USA
FSHW010316270721
83422FS